I0821201

Sign Language & Places

Bela Davis

Abdo Kids Junior
is an Imprint of Abdo Kids
abdobooks.com

abdobooks.com

Published by Abdo Kids, a division of ABDO, P.O. Box 398166, Minneapolis, Minnesota 55439.

Abdo Kids Junior™ is a trademark and logo of Abdo Kids.

Printed in the United States of America, North Mankato, Minnesota.

102024

012025

THIS BOOK CONTAINS RECYCLED MATERIALS

Photo Credits: Shutterstock

Production Contributors: Teddy Borth, Jennie Forsberg, Grace Hansen

Design Contributors: Candice Keimig, Pakou Moua

Library of Congress Control Number: 2024936610

Publisher's Cataloging-in-Publication Data

Names: Davis, Bela, author.

Title: Sign language & places / by Bela Davis

Description: Minneapolis, Minnesota : Abdo Kids, 2025 | Series: Everyday sign language set 3 | Includes online resources and index.

Identifiers: ISBN 9798384902782 (lib. bdg.) | ISBN 9798384903482 (ebook) | ISBN 9798384903833 (Read-to-me ebook)

Subjects: LCSH: American Sign Language--Juvenile literature. | Public spaces--Juvenile literature. | Deaf--Means of communication--Juvenile literature. | Language acquisition--Juvenile literature.

Classification: DDC 419--dc23

Table of Contents

Signs and Places

ASL is a visual language. There is a sign for all the places people like to go!

GO

1. Extend both pointer fingers on both hands while tucking the other fingers in
2. Start with the hands back toward the body, pointer fingers pointing up
3. Move the hands in an arc forward

Gabriel and his family bought a new home. He is excited to move in!

HOME

1. With one hand, touch the fingers and thumb together
2. Touch the tips of the fingers to the side of the mouth
3. Then touch the tips of the fingers to the top of the cheek

Ken loves finding new books at the library.

LIBRARY
1. Make the "L" sign
2. Bring hand to about shoulder height
3. Move hand in a circular motion

Emma goes down the slide at the park.

PARK (PLAY AREA)

A. First make the sign for "PLAY"
   1. Make both hands into fists with the pinkies and thumbs extended
   2. Twist both hands back and forth

B. Then sign "AREA"
   1. Take one flat hand, palm facing down
   2. Make horizontal circles

Jimmy and his sister have dessert at the restaurant.

RESTAURANT

1. With one hand, make the "R" sign
2. Bring the "R" hand to one side of the chin and slide it down, then touch the other side of the chin and slide it down

Luis and his aunt
shop at the mall.

SALE
MALL
1. Fingerspell M-A-L-L
M
A
L
L

Jessa likes to go down every aisle at the grocery store.

GROCERY STORE (FOOD STORE)

A. First make the sign for "FOOD/EAT"
   1. Using one hand, touch the thumb and fingers together
   2. Tap the tips of the fingers twice to the mouth

B. Then make the sign for "STORE"
   1. On both hands, touch the thumbs and fingers together
   2. Hold hands on either side of the body
   3. Shake the hands back and forth twisting at the wrist

The science museum has
a lot of fun things to see!

MUSEUM

1. Make the “M” sign with both hands
2. Outline the shape of a building by starting at the tip of the roof, moving downward at an angle, and then the vertical walls

The ASL Alphabet!

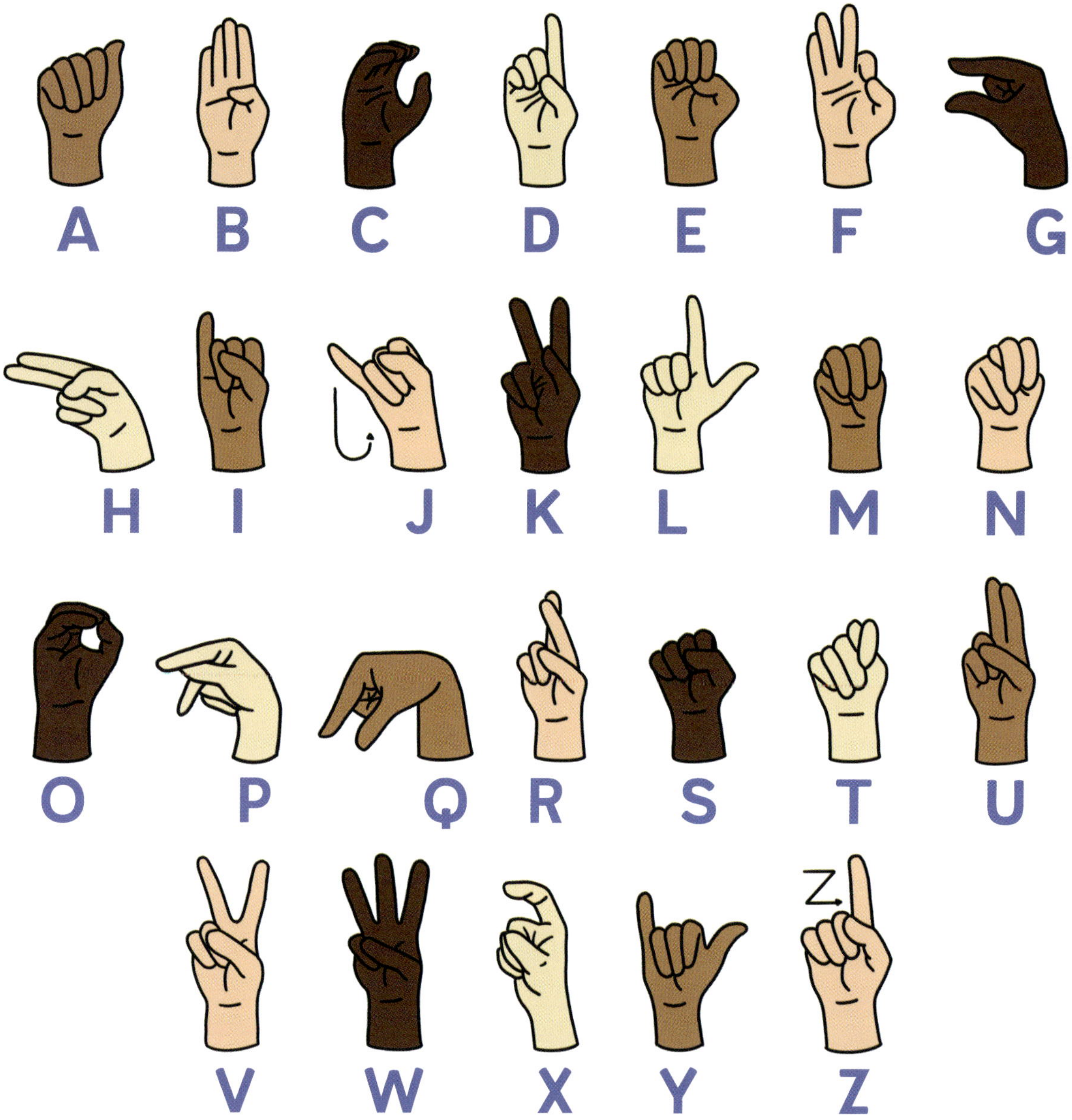

A B C D E F G

H I J K L M N

O P Q R S T U

V W X Y Z

Glossary

aisle

an open space for passing between rows or sections of seats or shelves.

ASL

short for American Sign Language, a language used by many deaf people in North America.

Index

Visit **abdokids.com** to access crafts, games, videos, and more!

Use Abdo Kids code

ESK2782

or scan this QR code!